All Will
Be Well

"So many in our culture are looking for 'spiritual teachers' today. Mere repetition of formulas is no longer enough to feed our hungry souls. Here is solid, traditional, and yet revolutionary spiritual teaching from the ages! As with all great wisdom, you will find yourself saying, 'I knew that . . . but I never heard it said so well, and I did not fully know it until this saint said it!'"

Richard Rohr, O.F.M.
Center for Action and Contemplation
Albuquerque, New Mexico

"These are glorious little books—concise and attractively designed! Distilled from the most influential writings in the Christian tradition, these pocket-sized books help you feel like you're having an intimate conversation with a wise counselor, a holy friend, or a beloved mentor. Give yourself a few minutes a day and let these holy men and women lead you to a closer relationship with the God who wants to be closer to you."

James Martin, S.J.
Author of *My Life with the Saints*

"The Great Spiritual Teachers series shows how surprisingly similar the struggles and frustrations of these teachers are to our own daily challenges and distractions. Their wisdom also reminds us that daily challenges bring opportunities for grace and invite God to be part of our day. These spiritual teachers can help us to turn prayer into conversation with God, and the most mundane occasions become meetings with God in our neighbors."

Dr. Carolyn Y. Woo
Distinguished President's Fellow for Global Development
Purdue University

All Will
Be Well

GREAT SPIRITUAL TEACHERS

30 Days with Julian of Norwich

AVE MARIA PRESS AVE Notre Dame, Indiana

Series Editor for the Great Spiritual Teachers: John Kirvan.

Originally published as *All Will Be Well: Based on the Classic Spirituality of Julian of Norwich,* edited by Richard Chilson for the 30 Days with a Great Spiritual Teacher series.

The writings of Julian of Norwich included in this book are paraphrased from *Showings*, sometimes called *Revelations of Divine Love*, first published in the fourteenth century.

Founded in 1865, Ave Maria Press is a ministry of the United States Province of Holy Cross.

www.avemariapress.com

ISBN-10 1-59471-151-8, ISBN-13 978-1-59471-151-0

Cover and text design by Katherine Robinson.

Cover art of Julian of Norwich © Ann Burt Devotional Art, www.etsy.com/shop/AnnBurtDevotionalArt.

Printed and bound in the United States of America.

Julian of Norwich understood the central message for spiritual life: God is love and it is only if one opens oneself to this love, totally and with total trust, and lets it become one's sole guide in life, that all things are transfigured, true peace and true joy found and one is able to radiate it.

—Pope Benedict XVI, General Audience, December 1, 2010

CONTENTS

TIMELINE

ca. 1325	The Renaissance begins in Italy.
1337–1453	The Hundred Years' War occurs between France and England as the two countries fight for control of France.
1342	Julian of Norwich is born in England.
1347–1351	The Black Death, or bubonic plague, sweeps through Europe, killing at least 25 million people.
1370	Pope Gregory XI is elected.
1373	Julian falls ill and is thought to be near death. While a curate administers last rites on May 8, Julian sees Jesus on the crucifix the curate is holding begin to bleed. She has fifteen visions over the course of the next few hours and has a sixteenth vision the following night. By May 13, Julian is completely recovered from her illness. Julian begins writing her *Short Text*, in which she detailed the visions she saw, shortly afterward. The *Short Text* is also known as the *Showings*.
1377	Pope Gregory XI returns the papal court to Rome, ending the Avignon papacy.
1378–1417	The Western Schism occurs, in which popes in Rome and France vie for control of the Catholic Church.

1381   The Peasants' Revolt occurs across England, partially as a result of the instability caused by the Black Death and the high taxes imposed on the English people to pay for the Hundred Years' War.

ca. 1390s While it is unknown when Julian first entered her cell, by this time, Julian is an anchoress. Julian begins an expansion of her *Short Text*, including a theological exploration of the meaning of her visions that focused especially on the theme of divine love and that frequently compared divine love to maternal love. This expanded edition is now known as the *Long Text* or *Revelations of Divine Love*.

1414   English mystic Margery Kempe visits Julian for spiritual advice. She later writes about her visit in *The Book of Margery Kempe*, the first autobiography written by a woman in English.

1414–1418 The Council of Constance is held. It ends the Western Schism by deposing or accepting the resignation of all papal claimants and, in 1417, electing Pope Martin V.

ca. 1416 Julian dies sometime after this year.

1470s   A scribe makes a copy of Julian's *Short Text*. This is the earliest surviving copy of the work.

1670   Serenus de Cressy translates the *Long Text*,
        which was originally written in Middle Eng-
        lish, and publishes it, making Julian's work
        available for the first time. Modern publica-
        tions of Julian's work are either based on
        Cressy's work or are updated translations
        of the *Long Text*, of which only three manu-
        script copies exist. One copy, the Paris Manu-
        script, resides in the Bibliothèque nationale
        de France, while the other two copies are
        held in the British Library.

1910   The copy of the *Short Text* made in the 1470s,
        thought lost since the mid-1700s, is found in
        a collection of manuscripts and is purchased
        by the British Museum. It is currently held in
        the British Library.

WHO IS JULIAN OF NORWICH?

For a mystic of such a great influence, we know precious little about Julian of Norwich. We do not even know whether Julian was her name, for she was an anchoress whose house was attached to the church of St. Julian in Norwich—whether she too was named Julian is anyone's guess. She lived in the late fourteenth century and is the first woman writer in English whose work survives. A contemporary of Chaucer, her prose is treasured for its grace and lucidity.

She has left us but one work, although in two versions. Known as the *Showings,* it describes visions which she had received from God and plumbs the meaning of these revelations. The major vision occurred in May 1373 and the first version, the shorter work, was written soon after that. The second and longer version was not written until some twenty years later. It expands upon the earlier work and delves more into the meaning of the visions. Our excerpts are drawn mostly from the expanded version.

But before proceeding, it might be good for us to have some idea of Julian's world. Although she was a recluse, she was not entirely apart from the world. She lived sealed in a cottage joined to the church in the city of Norwich. The modern fiction is that an anchorite was walled into a tiny church alcove with barely room for a *prie-dieu* and hard bed. Julian would probably have had a suite of rooms as well as a walled garden. Solitaries were even allowed to have cattle and property. They also had guests. The life was simple with much time devoted to prayer and contemplation, but it was not the cruel torture we might imagine.

A main road passed right outside her house and Julian gave spiritual direction and advice to the many people who sought her out. One of these was Margery Kempe, who while certainly not of Julian's sanctity, has entered history for writing the first biography of women in English. Nor was Julian entirely alone within her cottage. She would have had a maid (we know the names of two of them). And she may have had pets.

Norwich was a busy port in her time. And a time of trouble it was. The plague swept through the city repeatedly. Disease and bad weather produced famine. The church itself was wracked by the Western Schism with three competing popes. The Hundred Years War was raging. And when John Wycliffe and his followers called for reform in the church, they were burned as heretics. Some of them would have been led along the road in front of Julian's retreat on the way to their death. Julian, walled up though she was, was not sitting in an ivory tower.

Nor was she isolated from the learning of her time. An Augustinian friary was across the street from her house, and it would have been natural for her to borrow books and engage in conversation with the friars. There were women's communities in the area as well. In fact there might even have been a group known as Beguines—a women's movement that inspired reform in the church.

Julian sets her vision in context when she reported that she had asked three boons of God. First, she wished to remember Christ's passion in a special way. She did not ask to suffer as he suffered, but rather to enter into the feelings of a bystander. Second, she wanted to suffer from an illness so great that she and those around her would think it was mortal. By doing so, and coming through it, she felt that she would pass over and be able to devote herself entirely to the glory of God. Finally she wished for three wounds: "The wound of contrition, the wound of compassion, and the wound of longing with my will for God."

These wishes were granted. Julian spoke of her illness throughout *Showings*. And she was granted a vision of Christ's passion that she described vividly and eloquently. The three wounds gave her the grace to share her revelation with others.

As Julian reflected upon her experiences over the years, she became more and more willing to trust them and to use them almost as sacred texts along with the scriptures. Like many mystics her direct experience of God allowed her to correct the dominant spirituality of her day and align the Christian community more with the original revelation of Jesus.

Even to today's reader Julian provides a wonderful, joyous corrective to much of Christianity. While many Christians might fit into what William James called the unhealthy soul—seeing the world and God primarily in terms of sin and judgment—Julian is an example of the

healthy soul. For her, love and joy were paramount in
the experience of God. If you are approaching Julian
from a background of puritanical Christianity, whether
Protestant or Catholic, bear in mind that shocking as
some of her images and thoughts are, she is quite within the Catholic tradition.

Julian's great illness was a major conversion experience. All Christian conversion is primarily imaged
in terms of the death and resurrection paradigm. This
conversion begins with baptism, but hopefully continues throughout one's life. Any death experience is a
stripping away, a dying to one's past. The resurrection
out of death is a new beginning, and new beginnings
are uncluttered. The death experience forces one to
sort out the essential from the expendable. People
confronting life-threatening illness often undergo deep
conversion experiences.

They realize that their time is precious. If they want
to do something they should do it right away.

One could certainly maintain that Christian teaching in Julian's day, and even in our own day, is hardly uncluttered. Christians have so fussed over and
nuanced the good news that sometimes it is difficult
to see the gospel as liberating. The liberation comes in
resurrection. Julian's encounter with God put things in
perspective for her.

In the shorter version of *Showings*, she seems quite
reserved and unassuming around her revelations. But
by the time the final text was written, she was willing to

put them on a level with scripture. She trusted that God was truly revealing himself to her. This leads her not to contradict church teaching, but to refocus the emphasis upon salvation and love rather than on law and justice.

What does Julian offer the modern reader? First, she adds her voice to the growing reexamination of patriarchal images of God. She did not deny traditional teaching, but she added the dimension of God's role as mother and specifically applied it to Jesus. Christ nourishes us from his breasts. This metaphor is not without precedent in Jesus himself who used feminine imagery in speaking of the kingdom of God—a woman baking bread, a widow looking for a coin. He even referred to himself as a hen gathering her chicks under her wing. Patriarchal Christianity has not quarried these metaphors, but Julian exalted the feminine as a necessary corrective.

Even when she spoke of God's masculinity, she added an important image. She told about Christ's immense courtesy. Of course in her day, courtesy—or knowing how to act at court—was of tremendous importance. Yet only Julian applies this virtue to God. Today, many see God as almighty judge or awesome king. And so God is. But without this incredible courtesy, God becomes the tyrant of tyrants. Surely Jesus refutes such an assumption. God's courtesy makes God supremely respectful of us, patient with our failings, considerate of our freedom. It makes God incredibly appealing and close to us, as well. How can we not love a God who is so solicitous of us?

Julian's teaching on sin is also important today. For many, Christianity spends so much effort pondering sin. Sin almost seems more significant than grace. Although they would be loath to admit it, these Christians display an obsession with sin that suggests it abounds more than grace.

While sin is certainly real for Julian, it is not the preeminent reality. She is conscious of it primarily in herself. Over and over, she applies the words from her revelation that somehow in the mystery of God, "All will be well." She even wrestles with the teaching of the church about the damned. While not denying the possibility that some people will be damned, she trusts that Christ has all things in hand and will bring good out of all things.

Again, this is solid Catholic teaching. The church merely affirms that there must be the possibility of hell to allow for human freedom. God will not make people enter the kingdom against their will. But we do not have to believe that anyone has ever made the choice of denying the power of love.

Perhaps the most striking image in Julian's writing must be read between the lines. She tells us to think of ourselves as infants. When we have soiled ourselves, we do not descend into a pit of shame and blame. No, we run immediately to our mothers who welcome us, change our diapers, and then shower us with hugs and kisses to send us on our way. It is a humiliating image for an adult, but in that humility God's powerful love can be revealed to us.

Finally, Julian gives us the gift of joy. So much in Christianity wears a gloomy, sour face, yet the gospel is good news. God loves us so much that he even stooped to take on a human form and die for us. Wake up to the beauty and the love that oozes out of every moment in all of creation! Julian may have been an anchoress shut up in a cottage, but that cottage opened upon a walled garden as well as a busy street. The love of creation and human society fills her work. Her joy is contagious; it overflows. We can certainly profit from such a gracious and ecstatic voice in our anxious age.

Our selections are all drawn from the longer second version of the *Showings*. We have not included any of the revelations themselves, but rather their meanings and applications. This is not a translation but rather a paraphrase of her work. We have focused upon those aspects of her thought relevant to anyone interested in the spiritual life. Institutional references to church, dogma, and sacraments are minimized, and, although she understood her original readers to be baptized Christians, we have extended that audience to include all who seek love and life. This book is a threshold inviting us to become acquainted with one of the great mystics and writers of the English language. Hopefully, it will inspire you to go on to encounter Julian of Norwich first hand.

HOW TO USE
THIS BOOK

The books in the Great Spiritual Teachers series provide an introduction to the spiritual insights and wisdom of some of history's most extraordinary saints. Through these pages, you'll be accompanied by a spiritual teacher whose wisdom will awaken, enrich, and empower your walk with the Lord.

In other words, these books take you on a spiritual journey.

We have some suggestions for how you can make the most of this journey. But keep in mind that these books are meant to help you experience the freedom and joy of communing with God in prayer. The daily format is there to help—but don't hesitate to go at your own pace or take your own route! Repeat a day as often as you like, or skip a day if the reading isn't resonating with where you are in your journey. The goal is to hear the voice of God through the words of the saints.

However you choose to use this book, it's helpful to understand the thinking behind the format used for each day. We've chosen to follow the suggestion of the classic book on spirituality *The Cloud of Unknowing*, which describes a three-part movement of *reading*, *reflecting*, and *praying*: "These three are so linked together that there can be no profitable reflection without first reading or hearing. Nor will beginners or even the spiritually adept come to true prayer without first taking time to reflect on what they have heard or read."

Throughout these thirty days you'll follow in the footsteps of this longstanding tradition. Each day starts with a section called "My Day Begins," in which you'll find a passage quoted or adapted from a great spiritual teacher. This is followed by "All Through the Day," which provides a short, memorable phrase (drawn from or based on the reading) that you can carry with you throughout the day, enabling you to reflect and meditate on a key truth, question, or insight. In the final section, "My Day Is Ending," you're encouraged to find a quiet place to go to the Lord in prayer, drawing on that day's reading as you lift up your petitions and praises to him.

MY DAY BEGINS

One of the best ways you can begin your day is to put yourself in the company of a great spiritual teacher.

The selected passages are short—just a few hundred words. But they are powerful! They've been chosen specifically for their ability to provide spiritual focus for your day and to remind you that you are a spiritual being, intended for relationship and intimacy with God.

These morning readings don't just put you in the presence of a spiritual teacher who can accompany you on your journey—they are also designed to invite you into God's presence so you can start your day in conversation with him.

If you find that you don't fully understand the reading, don't be discouraged! For now, focus on your heart's response. Ask the Lord for wisdom and insight.

It's also helpful to read *slowly*. We've divided the
passages into sense lines to help you do just that.
Instead of rushing through the reading, savor each
word. Pay attention to which phrases or images resonate in your heart. Make room for God to speak. In
short, read prayerfully. Each day's opening reading is
meant to foster attentiveness to God and an attitude of
readiness to hear what he wants to say to you.

All Through the Day

After the day's reading you'll find a meditation that you
can reflect on throughout your day. As you move for-
ward with the busyness of everyday life, return to this
reflection as often as you can. Try writing it down on a
card and placing it somewhere you'll see it frequently.
Or copy it down in a journal or planner. Recite it in the
little free moments between tasks and conversations.

This reflection shouldn't take you out of the day's
responsibilities. Rather, it should serve as a gentle
reminder of God's presence within the many activities
and tasks that make up your day—and an expression of
your desire to live in connection with him.

My Day Is Ending

No matter what your day has brought to you, there's
great wisdom in reaching the end of it and turning
everything over to God in prayer, intentionally setting
your mind and heart on him, and listening for his voice.

If you find that it's not easy to let go of the events of the day, to find peace and closure and solace in God's presence, here are some suggestions to help you:

1. Find a quiet, distraction-free place that you can return to each evening.

2. Quiet your spirit. Sometimes this involves relaxing your body and letting go of physical tension. Focus on breathing deeply and deliberately.

3. When you feel calm and at peace, focus on the evening prayer phrase by phrase. If you find yourself getting caught up in analyzing specific words or becoming distracted, don't worry! Just pause, breathe, and begin again.

The time spent with the evening prayer doesn't need to be very long—just remember that it is a time of expressing complete trust and confidence in God, preparing yourself for a night of peaceful sleep. End the day as you began it, resting in his presence.

SOME OTHER WAYS TO USE THIS BOOK

1. *Create your own reflections.* If the provided reflection doesn't resonate with you, or if you'd like to add to it, choose another phrase or image from the morning reading that caught your attention.

2. *Incorporate journaling into your spiritual journey.* Many find that journaling—either through copying out the provided reflections and prayers or writing

your own—is an excellent way to slow down and focus. Or, you could use a journal to keep a record of your experiences on this thirty-day journey, such as the insights that had the biggest impact on your thinking, or any daily changes you noticed in your heart or behavior.

3. *Look for contrasts.* Sometimes two readings or reflections might seem to stand in tension with each other. Often, such tensions highlight areas for fruitful reflection. Write down the contrasting passages and any questions they raise. Meditate on them and pray about them—God may provide new illumination as you ponder!

4. *Form a small group.* You're not alone is seeking to deepen your spiritual life—so why not invite others to join you on your thirty-day journey? Try meeting weekly to discuss that week's readings, reflections, and prayers. Talk to each other about how God is working in your lives. Pray together.

We hope that you'll be richly blessed by the books in this series. As you intentionally fill your days with the words and wisdom of a great spiritual teacher, we pray that you'll be ushered daily into the divine presence, experiencing more deeply than ever the life-giving joy of intimacy with the God who loves you.

The Publisher

THIRTY DAYS WITH
JULIAN OF NORWICH

DAY ONE

My Day Begins

And God showed me a little thing,
in the palm of my hand,
round like a ball,
no bigger than a hazelnut.
I gazed at it, puzzling at what it might be.
And God said to me,
"It is all of creation."
I was amazed that it could last
and did not suddenly disintegrate
and fall into nothingness,
for it was so tiny.
And again God spoke to me,
"It lasts, both now and forever,
because I cherish it."
And I understood that everything has its being
owing to God's care and love.
We need to realize the insignificance of creation
and see it for the emptiness it is
before we can embrace the uncreated God in love.

We will find no rest for our heart or spirit
as long as we seek it in insignificant things,
which cannot satisfy us,
rather than in God,
who is omnipotent, omniscient, and beneficent.
He is our true repose.
And he desires to be known,
and is pleased that we should rest in him.
For nothing less than him can satisfy us.
We cannot rest
until we are detached from all that is created.
When we have done so
for love of God who is all,
only then are we able to enjoy spiritual rest.

ALL THROUGH THE DAY

Nothing less than God can satisfy us.

MY DAY IS ENDING

Take the image of the hazelnut.
What incidents in your life today seem as small and
insignificant as this hazelnut?

Imagine feeling God's concern and love for you
in these small things.
What small things distracted you
from the experience of God's love today?
When did you remember to rest in God today?

NIGHT PRAYER

Out of your goodness, Lord, give me yourself,
for you are sufficient for me, and I can ask
for nothing less that can render you full worship.
And if I ask for anything less, I am constantly lacking;
only in you do I possess everything.

My Day Begins

For just as our bodies are clothed in garments,
our flesh enclosed by our skin,
our bones wrapped in flesh,
our hearts centered in our body;
so are we, spirit and flesh,
clothed head to toe in the goodness of God.
But this metaphor hardly does justice,
for all these things will decline and wear out.
God's goodness, however, is everlasting,
and is incomparably nearer to us than our very flesh.
Our beloved wishes that our spirits might cling to him
with all our strength,
and never let go of his goodness.
No mere creature can ever imagine
just how dearly, sweetly, and tenderly
our Creator loves us.
So with his grace and aid,
let us spiritually rest in contemplation,
forever marveling
at the high, surpassing, single-minded,

immeasurable love
that our good Lord extends to us.
Doing so, we can dare ask our lover
for whatever we wish
because our wills naturally seek only God.
And God in turn desires only us.
And never can we stop
the desiring and longing
until he is ours in the fullness of bliss.
Above all else,
this fond gazing upon our Creator
makes us aware of our own insignificance,
fills us with awe and humility,
and with abounding love for our neighbor.

ALL THROUGH THE DAY

So are we, spirit and flesh, clothed head to toe,
in the goodness of God.

MY DAY IS ENDING

What was your humblest need today?
Did you sense God's presence there?
Remember this need and try to sense God's presence
and love there now.

How and when did you sense yourself clad and
enclosed in God's goodness today?
Spend a few moments now in contemplation:
God is adhering to you
and you in turn can adhere to God.

NIGHT PRAYER

Gentlest God, clasp me in your arms.
Show me your love for the least of me,
and inspire me in turn to such love
so that you become all my will,
all my love, and the fullness of my joy.

DAY THREE

My Day Begins

Our Lord desires
that our spirit be truly turned to gaze upon him
and upon all his glorious creation,
for it is exceedingly good.
And his judgments are sweet and comforting,
and bring our spirit to rest.
Thus, we turn from scrutinizing our own blind actions
toward the delightfulness of God.
For we consider some actions good
and others wrong,
but God does not look upon them so:
for God has made all things,
so all that is done
is in some way God's doing.
For it is easy to see
that the best actions are well done,
but the smallest actions also share this character,
because all things
have been accomplished

according to the nature and plan
ordered by God from the beginning.
No one acts but God.
God never changes his mind in anything,
and never will.
Nothing in creation
was unknown by him from the beginning.
All was set in order before anything was made.
Nothing will fail in its design,
for all is abundantly good.
So the Trinity is entirely pleased with all its works.
Behold, I am God.
Behold, I am in all things.
Behold, I accomplish all things.
Behold, I never withdraw my arms from my work.
Behold, I never fail to guide all things
toward the purpose for which I created them,
before time began,
with the strength, wisdom, and love,
with which I created all.
So how can anything go wrong?

ALL THROUGH THE DAY

Behold, I never withdraw my arms from my work.

My Day Is Ending

Recall something today
that you thought went poorly at the time.
In your imagination, now picture it ultimately
going well, as it is in God's care.
Is there something from your past that you felt at one
time to be a failure? Can you now see that
God was working toward a good end?
What do you think failed for you today?
Take it to God in prayer.
Ask God to comfort you in the rightness of
what happened.
Be relaxed in this meditation;
don't push too hard. Let God comfort you.

Night Prayer

Most wonderful Lover.
Help me to see that you are God.
To see how you are in all things.
To have confidence that you do all things.
To trust that you never abandon your work.
Guide me and all creation to the end
you have ordained for us, before time began.
I have confidence you will do so

with the same power, wisdom, and love
with which you made us.
Convince us more deeply
that nothing in you can be amiss.

DAY FOUR

MY DAY BEGINS

Now our Lord reminded me
of the desire for him I had earlier.
I saw that nothing stood in my way but sin,
and I realized that this is the same for all of us.
And I thought that if there were no sin,
we would all be pure and akin to our Lord
just as we had been created sinless.
But in my vision, Jesus informed me
of everything necessary for me to know.
And he told me: Sin is necessary,
but everything will turn out for the good,
and all will be well,
and everything will be well.
By the simple word, "sin"
God reminded me of all that is not good
and of the suffering and grief of all creation,
and above all of the utter shame and sacrifice
he endured for our salvation.
We have all suffered woe and sorrow
as we follow our master Jesus,

and we shall do so until we are utterly purified.
I did not see sin itself,
for it has no real substance,
it is not real;
it can be known only by the suffering it causes,
and even that pain lasts but a while.
And during the woe
we might take consolation in our Lord's suffering.
And out of his tender love, he consoles us, saying:
True, sin caused this pain, but all will be well.
In his voice I never hear a hint of blame,
and since we who are guilty are not blamed,
why should we in turn blame God?

ALL THROUGH THE DAY

Sin is necessary, but all will be well.

MY DAY IS ENDING

Today, did you look at something as sin,
as something that hindered your relation with God?
Imagine how it might work out well in the end
following Julian's insight.
Consider some of the sins of our world
such as war and pollution.

How might these sins draw us closer to God?
How might they awaken us to our precarious condition
and help us to turn toward God?
Can you see the sins and failings of this day as a lack?
Julian says that sin has no kind of substance.
How can you see this in your own sins and failings?

NIGHT PRAYER

God our Comforter,
show me how you guide me through my life
not only in my joys and virtues, but even when
I choose wrong paths and am weak.
Give us hope that in the midst of denial and darkness,
your love still holds us readily and sweetly,
guiding us home.

DAY FIVE

My Day Begins

And I beheld Christ's mercy upon us
on account of our sin.
And just as previously,
I was filled with sorrow and pity
because of Christ's suffering.
So, now I was moved with compassion
on behalf of my neighbors,
the servants of God,
who are all greatly loved and saved.
For our community is shaken
by grief, anguish, and woe,
as you would shake a rag in the wind.
And I began to understand
how our Lord could rejoice
with sympathy and compassion
over the afflictions of his people.
He visits something upon each one he loves,
in order to bring us to happiness.
Although this thing carries no blame in his eyes,
we are scorned and rejected by the world because of it.

Jesus wishes us to realize that it will be converted to
our glory and that we will benefit by the strength
of his suffering.
Nor do we endure distress alone,
but are united to him.
We behold in him the ground of our being.
And we realize that his suffering and affliction
so far surpass anything we might endure
that we cannot fully comprehend it.
When we come to see this, we will stop
weeping and lamenting our own sufferings.
We will begin to understand
that our sufferings are well deserved,
but his love always excuses us.
Out of his great courtesy
he never censures us,
but instead looks upon us
with compassion and sympathy,
seeing us as righteous children without guilt.

ALL THROUGH THE DAY

Out of his great courtesy, he never censures us.

MY DAY IS ENDING

Call to mind Christ's passion
and unite it in your imagination
with any pain that you have suffered today.
Imagine these together, working for the healing
of the world.
Who are those in pain for whom you compassionately
reach out?
Call them to mind now and unite them also
to the passion of Christ and to your own suffering.
Recall any defects that
you may have experienced during the day,
and imagine them to be of no account in Christ's sight.
Let them go.
Drop them into the passion of Christ.

NIGHT PRAYER

Most courteous Lord,
may my sins, defects, and sufferings
be joined to your Passion.
Help me to bear misunderstanding,
prejudice, and rejection, knowing that they will
be healed.

Give me faith that all pains will be turned
to our honor and profit and will culminate in
bliss and joy.

DAY SIX

My Day Begins

God wants us to be enfolded in repose and peace.
Only then shall Christ's spiritual thirst be satisfied.
This is his thirst: a desire to love us.
That love shall continue until the last day,
when we shall be completely gathered
into his joy and happiness.
He yearns to integrate us into himself in bliss.
For we are not yet as fully immersed in him
as we shall be.
Christ Jesus is both human and divine.
Because he is divine, he is supreme happiness.
So he was from the beginning, and
so shall he be until the ending.
This happiness can neither increase nor diminish.
Because he is human as well as divine, he
suffered and died out of love to bring us to bliss.
And he takes joy in these deeds of his humanity.
For he told me:
It gives me joy, bliss, and eternal delight
to have suffered for you.

This is the satisfaction he receives from his work.
As Christ is our head,
he is glorious and invincible.
And as he is the body in which we are all conjoined,
he is not yet wholly glorified or invincible.
He still carries that same thirst
that he had upon the cross.
And he shall continue to suffer it
until the last spirit has been brought up to join him.
Because he yearns for us, we in turn ache for him.
No one comes to bliss without such an ache.
This thirst springs from God's eternal goodness
just as compassion does.
So he is compassionate toward us
and desires to possess us.
But his wisdom and love
will not allow the end to come
before the time is ripe.

ALL THROUGH THE DAY

Because he yearns for us, we, in turn, ache for him,
and no one comes to bliss without it.

MY DAY IS ENDING

Recall times during this day
when you felt some yearning for wholeness.
Were you able to connect your own yearning
with that of God yearning for you in turn?
Were there moments of peace and rest for you today?
Recall them now, and spend a few moments
savoring them.
See if, in your recollection,
you can make them even more peaceful.
And imagine, as well,
how much more peaceful you might be in the future.
Take time to relax and enjoy this meditation.

NIGHT PRAYER

Dear Lord, thank you for the glimpses of
peace and rest
you have provided today.
Help me to know your longing for me,
and aid my desire to turn to you above all else.
In my sorrow, give me assurance that you suffer
with me
and that eventually we shall be together
in complete happiness.

DAY SEVEN

MY DAY BEGINS

On one occasion, our good Lord told me:
every kind of thing will be all right.
He desires us to understand
that not only does he concern himself
with great and noble things,
but equally with small and simple things.
We too should realize
that the smallest thing will not be forgotten.
Now, there are many acts committed
that to us seem so evil and so harmful
that we despair of any good resulting from them.
While we are in sorrow and mourning concerning
these, we cannot relax in God's exalted and
wondrous wisdom.
For our reason is now so blinded, weak, and ignorant
that we cannot see
the Trinity's strength and goodness.
So God tells us:
You will yourself behold that all will be well.
It is as though he were telling us:

Take it now in faith and trust,
and in the end you will see truly, in all fullness
and joy. The Trinity will accomplish an action
on the last day.
What it will be and how it will be accomplished
no creature lower than Christ knows.
And so shall it remain veiled
until the act is accomplished.
And he wishes us to know this
so that our spirits
might be surrendered peacefully into his love,
and we might then ignore
every disturbance
which thwarts our true rejoicing in God.

ALL THROUGH THE DAY

The smallest thing will not be forgotten.

MY DAY IS ENDING

Think of a time today
when you forgot today's mantra,
when you felt forgotten.
In memory now bring it to today's phrase
and sit with it, knowing that God holds all in love.

Is there something that happened today
that strikes you as useless and counterproductive?
Do you feel that no good can come of it?
Remember it now, and in faith bring it to God.
Let God assure you of its hidden significance.
Can you remember some incident from the past
that you felt to be no good or even evil?
Can you now see this as a stepping stone
along your spiritual journey?

NIGHT PRAYER

Dear Lord, help me to trust in your wisdom
that nothing is forgotten.
Give me the strength to meet the events of my life,
believing that in you all will be revealed
and everything will be made well.
Help me to surrender my anxiety
so that my spirit might have ease
and be at peace in love.

MY DAY BEGINS

This is the great act
intended by our Lord God from eternity,
treasured and hidden in his heart,
known only to himself.
By this act he will make all things well.
For just as the blessed Trinity
made everything from nothing,
just so will the same Trinity
make everything wrong to be well.
And I was overcome with wonder at this:
our faith is grounded in God's word,
and whoever believes in that word
will be preserved completely.
Now holy doctrine tells us
that many creatures will be damned.
And if this is true,
it seemed impossible to me
that everything should be well,
as our Lord had shown me by revelation.
And in regard to this
I had no other answer but this:

"What is impossible for you
is not impossible for me.
I shall honor my word in everything,
and I shall make everything well."

So I was instructed by God's grace
to hold steadfastly to the faith,
and, at the same time,
to believe firmly
that everything will turn out for the best.
For this is the great action
that our Lord will accomplish,
and in this action he will keep his word entirely.
And what is not well
shall be made well.

ALL THROUGH THE DAY

What is impossible for you is not so for me.

MY DAY IS ENDING

What seemed most impossible today?
Bring it to God now in prayer,
and surrender it to his wisdom.
Were there times today when you were tempted
or did not trust at all?

Did you bring the mantra into the situation?
Did you forget about the reading entirely?
Do not enter into judgment.
Simply observe how you acted—
with no blame, no regret.
Just be curious about how you dealt with the moment.

NIGHT PRAYER

Dear Lord,
thank you for sharing your plan with us
that you will keep your word in everything.
Help me to trust in your words
and to let go of things that are beyond me.
May I find the faith
to surrender the impossible to you
so that I have more time to enjoy
the many beauties with which you visit me.

DAY NINE

MY DAY BEGINS

Sin is the sharpest scourge
that can strike anyone's spirit.
This scourge wears down both man and woman,
making them loathsome in their own sight.
It is not long until they consider themselves suited
only to hell,
until the Holy Spirit's touch
moves them to contrition
and turns bitterness into hope in God's mercy.
Then the Spirit begins to heal the wounds,
revive the spirit,
and return the person to life.
Dearly does our Lord protect us in his loving care
when we seem to be almost forsaken
and cast away on account of our sin.
And indeed we deserve as much.
Yet because of the humility we acquire in this fashion,
we are raised high in God's sight through his grace.
Contrition makes us clean,

compassion renders us ready,
and desire for God makes us worthy.
So all shame is transformed into joy and glory.
For our courteous Lord does not wish his
creatures to lose hope
even if they fall frequently and grievously.
Our failure does not prevent him from loving us.
Peace and love are always present within us,
living and laboring, but we unfortunately
do not always abide in peace and love.

ALL THROUGH THE DAY

Our failure does not prevent him from loving us.

MY DAY IS ENDING

Can you remember instances in the past
when your own pain and awareness of your faults
have opened you up to compassion for others?
Relive that moment now through memory.
Recall a time today when peace and love
definitely did not seem present for you.
In your imagination, relive this event
in the knowledge that God's peace and love

were truly present,
even though you were unaware of it.

NIGHT PRAYER

Courteous Lord Jesus,
help us to acknowledge and accept
all our failings, sins, and weaknesses,
trusting that you use them to our good
and through them draw us closer to you.
May our contrition make us clean,
may our compassion make us ready,
and may our longing for you make us worthy.
At all times, preserve us in the knowledge
that your peace and love abide always in us,
living and working, even when we have no feeling of
peace or love.

DAY TEN

MY DAY BEGINS

God wants us to understand prayer.
First, we must know through whom
and how our prayer begins.
So, he told me:
"I am the foundation."
Second, he wishes to teach us how to pray best.
Our will should be conformed joyfully to God's will.
Third, he desires us
to know the fruit and outcome of our prayer,
to be united and similar to our Lord in all things.
God intends our prayer and trust to be magnanimous.
If we do not trust as much as we pray,
we do not honor God fully,
and we place obstacles in our path.
This happens because we do not realize
that God himself is the ground of our praying.
Our very ability to pray is a gift of his loving grace.
We cannot ask for mercy and grace
unless they have first been extended to us.
Sometimes, it seems after praying a long time

that we have received no answer.
We should not let this disturb us.
God simply wishes
us to wait for a more suitable time,
or for more grace, or for a better gift.
Furthermore,
just as we experience God drawing us to him,
so we should pray that we will be drawn toward him.
It is not sufficient to do one without the other.
If we pray, but do not see that God is at work,
we become dejected and downcast
and so do him no honor.
And if we see him at work, but do not pray,
we do less than our duty.
But to see that he works, and to pray that he works,
gives God worship and benefits us.
When we pray thus, we will think we have
done nothing.
But if we do what we can, seeking mercy and grace,
we shall discover in him all that is deficient in us.

ALL THROUGH THE DAY

You are the ground of my prayer.

MY DAY IS ENDING

Look back over your day in terms of trust.
Were there times when you felt able to trust God or
another person?
Were there times when such trust was lacking?
Relive an incident now,
imagining a fullness of trust present.
How does it change the experience?
Spend some time contemplating God
as the very foundation from which prayer springs.
Visualize prayer flowing from this ground into you
and back to God.
When you pray in the future,
you might begin your prayer with this short
visualization.
Use it as a gateway into prayer.

NIGHT PRAYER

Lord, teach me to pray
and trust more fully in you.
Give me assurance
that you are with me always,
and teach me to be content
with the plan you have for me
and all your creatures.

DAY ELEVEN

My Day Begins

In his merciful way,
our good Lord always leads us
as long as we inhabit this impermanent life.
I saw no anger other than humanity's,
and God forgives us that,
for anger is no more
than perverse opposition to peace and love.
It arises from a lack of strength,
or wisdom, or goodness.
And this failure lies in ourselves
rather than in God.
Our sin and desperation
generate in us a wrath
and a continual opposition to peace and love.
But the ground of mercy is love,
and the ministry of mercy is to preserve us in love.
For mercy works in love,
with generosity, compassion, and sweetness.
And mercy labors within us,
preserving us, and converting everything to the good.

Through love, mercy allows us to fail,
at least in part, and to the extent that we fail, we fall.
To the extent that we fall, we die.
For we die without fail
when we no longer see and feel God, who is life.
Our failure is frightful,
our falling inglorious,
our dying wretched.
Yet never does love's compassionate eye turn from us,
nor does the operation of mercy cease.

ALL THROUGH THE DAY

Never does love's compassionate eye turn from us.

MY DAY IS ENDING

Review your day,
and focus particularly upon moments of anger.
Do not condemn yourself for the anger.
But with curiosity, ask yourself
whether the anger could have been caused
by a lack of power, wisdom, or goodness.
Bring God's mercy to your moments of anger.
Let the mercy touch each moment.
There is no need to force a healing.

Simply allow the mercy
to touch each moment of anger.
Let what happens or does not happen simply be.
Have no goal in this exercise except the process itself.

NIGHT PRAYER

Loving Father, I bring to you all my faults
and especially my wrath.
I see my anger leads to a dreadful failing,
a shameful falling, and a sorrowful dying.
But in this dying, I trust your mercy to
continually work to protect me,
even against myself,
and to turn everything to good for us.

DAY TWELVE

My Day Begins

And I saw in my visions
that God never has to forgive us
because he is incapable of becoming angry!
For all life is founded in love
and without that love, life is impossible.
Wrath and amity are inherently opposed.
And since God relieves and takes away our anger,
by which he humbles and tames us,
he himself must surely be loving, humble, and gentle.
And so, God's response is quite the opposite of angry.
We shall not be safe and blessed
until we abide in peace and love.
This is what salvation means.
And I beheld God as our genuine peace.
He is our protector when we ourselves are disturbed,
and he continually labors to bring us to rest.
But we shall not experience this peace
until we are wholly content with God,
and at love and peace
with both self and neighbor.

For contention is the cause of all our trouble and woe.
Our Lord Jesus takes trouble and woe from us
and raises them up where they become
more sweet and pleasurable
than heart can think or tongue tell.
And when we come home, we shall find them there,
turned entirely into beauty and love.

ALL THROUGH THE DAY

All life is founded in love and without that love,
life is impossible.

MY DAY IS ENDING

Recollect some moments of peace in your life today.
Let them expand in your imagination.
Be aware of that peace as a resting in God.
Can you remember moments of contrariness as well?
How did things progress from them?
Did they lead to tribulation and woe,
or did they lead to something else?
How did you respond to your contrariness?
Do not judge yourself.
Just be curious as to how you acted and what resulted.

NIGHT PRAYER

Dear God,
in your endless friendship
thank you for being patient with me.
Help me to be patient with myself.
Let me see my contrariness
as leading me closer to your love and peace.
Thank you for your presence
in the midst of my disquiet
I know it will be turned into true beauty
and endless love.

MY DAY BEGINS

Our Father's pity and compassion were for Adam,
his loved creature, when he fell.
His joy and happiness were for his dearly loved Son,
who is equal with the Father.
The merciful gaze of his face
ranged over all the world,
and descended with Adam into hell,
and this unceasing compassing
preserved Adam from eternal death.
This same mercy and compassion abide with us
until we are drawn up to heaven.
But we are blinded in this life,
and cannot behold God, our Father, as God is.
And when out of his kindness
he desires to show himself to us,
he shows himself in great simplicity,
as a human being.
However, I saw quite clearly
that we should not assume
that the Father is a creature.

But his sitting on the bare and wasted earth
means this: God made our spirit
to be his own city and resting place.
Of all creation
this is most pleasing to him.
And when we had fallen into grief and suffering,
we were not suited to that noble office.
But our kind Father
would not ready any other place to dwell.
Instead, he sat upon the ground,
waiting for humanity,
itself mixed with clay,
until such time as through grace,
his beloved son had restored to this city
its noble beauty
through his tremendous labor.

ALL THROUGH THE DAY

The merciful gaze of his face ranged over all the world.

MY DAY IS ENDING

God reveals himself to us in the human face and form.
How did you catch a sense of God today in the people
you met?

Call up the image of God,
sitting on the barren ground in exile
awaiting Christ to bring back his city—our spirit.
Join with the longing, passion, and love of God
in this exile.
Simply remain with this image in your heart
for a time.
Let it reveal God's endless love for humanity
and for you in particular.

NIGHT PRAYER

Dearest friend,
help me sense your longing for me.
May your exile from the human spirit
inspire in me an equal desire
for your presence within me.
And I give thanks for Jesus, your son,
who by his hard work,
has brought back your city, my spirit,
into its noble place of beauty.

DAY FOURTEEN

My Day Begins

Our life in this world
consists of a wondrous mixture of good and bad.
We contain within us
both our risen Lord Jesus Christ,
as well as the misery and woe of Adam's sin.
Protected by Christ, although dying,
we are touched by his grace
and raised to hope of salvation.
Afflicted by Adam's fall,
as well as our own sinfulness and woe,
we feel so benighted and blinded
that we can scarcely find any comfort.
But in our hearts, we trust in God
and hope in his mercy and grace,
for they are truly at work in us.
And our good God opens the eye of our understanding
so that we might see,
sometimes more, sometimes less,
according to the ability God gives us to receive it.
Now we are raised up to one,

now allowed to fall to the other.
And this fluctuation is so confusing
that we hardly know where we stand,
whether we consider ourselves or our fellows.
But what a marvelous confusion!
And it continues throughout our life.
But God wants us to trust that he is always with us.
He accompanies us in three ways:
in heaven, where in his rising he raises us
up with him;
on earth, where he leads us day by day;
and in our innermost being, where he constantly
dwells to guide and preserve us.
And this is our comfort—that we know in faith
that Christ is constantly with us.
Knowing this, we shall never succumb to the
pain and woe,
but always hope for another glimpse of his presence.

ALL THROUGH THE DAY

God wants us to trust that he is always with us.

MY DAY IS ENDING

Did you experience a marvelous mixture
of both well-being and woe today?
Recall it to mind now.
If you have no experience from today,
recall some past event.
This is not a pleasant experience, but it is life.
Sense in this experience a faith
that all is truly in God's hands and power.
If you experienced today
the darkness and blindness Julian speaks of,
recall that event now.
See whether you were able to wait for God then,
or, if you can reimagine the event now.
Place at the center a waiting for God.

NIGHT PRAYER

Jesus, my protector, hear my complaints, my pains,
my woes.
Show yourself to me in my darkness.
Increase my hope and trust in you.
Help me to sense and feel your presence
in my confusion and blindness.
Give me confidence that through your cross,
this unpalatable mixture will work to my good.

MY DAY BEGINS

Our spirit is made by God,
but it is made of nothing that is created.
This is how it is:
when God made our bodies,
he took the dirt of the earth.
Dirt is a substance mixed with all sorts of
earthly things,
and from this, he created our bodies.
But when God went to create our spirits,
he took nothing.
He simply created our souls.
Thus, created nature is truly joined to God, its maker,
who is essential nature and uncreated.
Consequently, nothing at all
can come between God and our spirits.
And by this eternal love, our spirits are
preserved whole.
In this eternal love,
God guides and protects us,
and we shall never be lost.

God desires us to understand
that the spirit is alive.
His goodness and grace assure us
that this life will last forever as we
love him, thank him, praise him.
And just as we were made for eternity,
so we are valued and enclosed in God,
known and loved from before time began.
So God desires us to know
that humanity is the best creature ever made,
and our complete expression and model
is the blessed spirit of Christ.
In addition, he desires us to know
that our beloved spirits
were wondrously knitted to him
in their creation
by a union so skillful and strong
that we are joined in God
and made holy forever.

ALL THROUGH THE DAY

Nothing at all can come between God and our spirits.

MY DAY IS ENDING

Can you recall any moments today
when you felt led and protected by God?
Did you experience this at the time?
Can you see it this way now?
Look back over your day
and see it completely bathed in God's love.
Include especially moments
when you may have felt far from such love.
Reimagine them now
as Julian encourages us to do.

NIGHT PRAYER

Beloved One,
thank you for calling me into being
and holding me in your love.
Help me to feel how preciously
I am knitted to you.
Make me aware of the knot of love
that ties you to me,
so I may courageously do your will.

DAY SIXTEEN

MY DAY BEGINS

Because of God's great love for humanity,
he does not make a distinction in love
between Christ and the least creature.
It is easy enough to believe
that the blessed Spirit of Christ
is high in the glorious Godhead;
but, as I have seen,
where the blessed Spirit of Christ dwells,
there dwell in him the spirits of all who will be saved.
So let us rejoice greatly
that God dwells within us.
Let us rejoice even further
that we dwell within God.
For our spirits are made to be God's resting place,
and our spirits' rest is in God who is unmade.
Great it is to know in our hearts
that God, who is our Maker,
rests in our spirits.
But far greater is it to know in our hearts,
our spirits, which are made, rest in God.

By that substance, God,
we are who we are!
I beheld no difference
between God and our substance.
All was God, as it were.
Yet, I knew that our substance is in God.
In other words,
God is God,
and we are creatures in God.

ALL THROUGH THE DAY

Our spirit is made to be God's resting place.

MY DAY IS ENDING

Julian says that "God dwells in our soul,"
and also that "our soul dwells in God."
Take each phrase in turn,
and look back over your day recalling times
when one or the other described your experience.
What is your experience?
God makes no distinction between Christ
and the least soul.

Reimagine your day now
and see everyone who was with you in this day caught
up in the same love of Christ.
Especially focus upon people
whom you might be tempted to call least,
those who do not have an easy entry
to your own love and compassion.

NIGHT PRAYER

Beloved Friend,
I rejoice in your intimacy with me.
Remove all the barriers that stand between us.
I welcome you into my heart;
let me make you at home there.
And let me see all other creatures joined together
in our love and intimacy.

DAY SEVENTEEN

MY DAY BEGINS

I saw with utter certainty
that it is faster and easier for us to come to know
God than to know our own spirits.
For our spirit is so deeply set in God
and so endlessly valued
that we cannot hope to know it
until we first know God, our Creator,
to whom we are united.
God is nearer us than our own spirit.
For God is the ground upon which we stand,
and God is the means
by which our essence and sensuality
are united in such a way
that we may never be separated.
Our spirit dwells in God as its true rest,
and stands in God as its true strength,
and is rooted in God as its eternal love.
So if we wish to come to know our own spirit,
if we wish to have communion with it,
we must seek it in God in whom it is enclosed.

With certainty
I saw that our longing will be accompanied by sorrow
until we are led so deeply into God
that we do indeed know our own spirit.
Our Lord himself leads us
into these lofty depths
with the same love by which he made us and saved us
through the mercy and grace of his death.
And we will never fully know God
until we come to know ourselves thoroughly.
For our spirit reaches its full flowering
when our sensuality has been lifted up
to the level of our essence
through the virtue of Christ's death,
enriched by the trials God sends to us
in mercy and grace.

ALL THROUGH THE DAY

God is nearer to us than our own spirit.

MY DAY IS ENDING

Take a few moments to reflect on the mystery
of yourself.

Julian says that we cannot know our own soul
except through God.
How might knowing God as your true source
change your self-image?
We tend to think of ourselves
as apart from others and from God.
Spend some time contemplating Julian's vision
that God is the foundation upon which our soul stands.
God is closer to us than we are to ourselves.
How might such an understanding influence
your outlook and behavior?

NIGHT PRAYER

Courteous God,
be the foundation of my being.
May I sit in you in true rest,
stand in you in sure strength,
and be rooted in you in endless love?
Reveal yourself more to me
so that I may know my true nature better
and act as I truly am.

DAY EIGHTEEN

MY DAY BEGINS

As for our essence,
God created us so noble and rich
that we always work in his will and for his glory.
Indeed I saw that we are his beloved,
and that we do what pleases him, continually,
and without cease.
And we are able to do this
by the great wealth and nobility given our spirits
when they were infused into our bodies.
Through this union we are made sensual.
In our essence we lack nothing,
but in our sensuality we fail,
although God will make good this failing
through his mercy and grace,
richly flowing into us from God's innate goodness.
I saw that from the beginning
God knows fully all the works
that he has or will ever accomplish.
He created the human race out of love,
and out of love he willed to take on our human nature.

Faith is the next gift we receive,
and from faith all blessings flow.
Faith springs out of the riches
with which our essence endows our sensitive souls.
God's goodness working through mercy and grace
plants this faith in us, and plants us in faith.
From faith flow all good things
by which we are guided and saved.
The virtues
that God's goodness draws from our essence
are gifts of the Holy Spirit,
who works through mercy
and restores through grace.
These virtues and gifts
are our treasure in Jesus Christ.
In the Virgin's womb
when God united himself to our humanity
he took also our sensuality.
And Christ who unites himself with everyone
is perfect humanity.

All Through the Day

We do what pleases him, continually and
without ceasing.

MY DAY IS ENDING

When today did you feel God's love?
When might it have helped you
to sense more keenly God's love for you?
What is your own view of your sensuality?
How have you experienced God through your
senses today?
Is your search for God limited to the intangible?
How might you find God
in touch? smell? taste? sight? sound?

NIGHT PRAYER

Constant Friend,
you are nearer than my very self.
Help me to feel your pleasure in all your creation.
Restore and fill what I lack
by the operation of your mercy and grace,
plentifully flowing into me
from your own natural goodness.
In your kindness,
show me how you have taken up my soul,
enclosed me entirely in yourself,
and united us forever in love.

MY DAY BEGINS

We are blessed through mercy and grace,
but we would be ignorant of this goodness
were it not opposed.
For evil was allowed to rise up against goodness,
and then mercy and grace rose up against evil
and turned it to the good.
It is God's wisdom to set good against evil.
So Jesus who sets good against evil is our mother.
We owe him our very being
for this motherhood
and all the delightful protection that follows after.
For as surely as God is father,
so surely is God also mother.
He shows this in all,
but particularly in these sweet words:

"I am the strength and goodness of the father,
I am the wisdom of the mother,
I am light, grace, and lovely love,
I am Trinity and unity;
I am the innate goodness of every creature,

I draw you toward love,
I endow you with longing;
I am the endless completion of all desiring."
So Jesus is our true mother by nature
because he has created us.
He is also our mother by grace,
for he took our created nature upon himself.
All the lovely deeds and tender services of motherhood
may be seen in him.
And I came to understand
three ways of looking at the motherhood of God.
First, our being is made through God.
Second, in Christ our nature is educated,
and thus begins the motherhood of grace.
Third, the motherhood of work flows out from God,
covering all with that same grace,
whose length, breadth, height, and depth
endures forever and ever.
And so is God's love.

ALL THROUGH THE DAY

I draw you toward love, and I endow you with longing.

MY DAY IS ENDING

How have you loved God today?
How might you have loved God?
Consider how you have experienced God
as father today.
How have you encountered God as mother?
What difference does it make in
how you relate to God
when you consider God as mother?

NIGHT PRAYER

Dear God,
power and goodness of fatherhood,
wisdom of motherhood,
light and grace which is all blessed love,
Trinity and unity,
make me long for you,
enable me to love you, and
inspire me to seek you
as the fulfilling of all true desires.

DAY TWENTY

MY DAY BEGINS

A mother's service
is the most intimate, willing, and dependable,
because it is the most natural,
as well as the most loving.
Certainly, it is the truest service we know.
And the only one who can perform this service
to its fullest is our Lord Jesus.
We know that our own mothers bore us
in suffering and death.
But what does our true mother do?
Only he, all loving, bears us for joy and endless life.
So he carried us within himself in love and pain,
until the fullness of time came
when he suffered the sharpest thorns
and most daunting pains.
And then, at the end, he died.
But even when this was over,
and even when we are carried to eternal bliss,
his everlasting love is still not content.
I saw this in his wondrous words of love:

"If I could have suffered more,
I would have."
He can die no more,
but that does not stop him.
He longs to feed us—
an obligation of his motherly love for us.
The human mother suckles her child with her own
milk, but Mother Jesus nourishes us with himself,
with the utmost courtesy, in the blessed sacrament.
This is the priceless food of eternal life.
And through all the sacraments,
he accompanies us upon our journey
with mercy and grace.
Our human mother may place us tenderly at her
breast, but Mother Jesus leads us into her breast
through the wound in her side,
where we glimpse both Godhead and heavenly joy
and are made certain of eternal happiness.

ALL THROUGH THE DAY

Mother Jesus nourishes us with himself.

MY DAY IS ENDING

How have you experienced God as mother today?
Julian sees the passion of Jesus
as the birth pangs of a mother.
How might God have suffered
so that you might be born this day?
How has Jesus nourished you today?
Looking back now,
are there other places and ways
in which you might have eaten the food of Christ?

NIGHT PRAYER

Devoted Mother,
I thank you for rebirthing me to life.
I give thanks
for the food which is yourself
given as my daily bread.
You nourish me into health and life
through your ministrations,
into power and grace through your word,
and into goodness through your holy community.

My Day Begins

The mother may, at times,
allow her child to fall
and to learn the hard way, for his own benefit.
Since she loves this child so,
she would never allow any real danger
to threaten her child.
And although earthly mothers have been known
to let their children die,
our heavenly Mother Jesus
would never allow us, his children, to perish.
He alone is all-mighty, all-wise, all-loving.
But often when we realize our faults
and our wretchedness,
we are so scared and filled with shame
that we don't know what to do.
Then our patient mother
doesn't want us to run away.
Nothing would please him less.
But then, he wishes us to behave just like a child.

When a child is terrified and frightened,
he runs to his mother as fast as he can.
If he can do nothing else,
he yells out to her for help.
With a child's humility
let us call out:
"Dear Mother, be sorry for me.
I've gotten myself into a filthy mess,
and I need your assistance and wisdom."
Even if we don't feel immediate relief,
we can be sure that Jesus is behaving as a wise mother.
For if he considers it beneficial that we mourn and
weep, his compassion and pity allow that
until the time is right. He permits it because
he loves us.
He wishes us to imitate the child
who naturally trusts in his mother's love
whatever the situation.
Our mother's hands continually surround us
to protect us.
Our Lord is like a good-hearted nurse
whose only job is to see to the safety of her charge.

ALL THROUGH THE DAY

He wishes us to behave just like a child.

My Day Is Ending

How did it feel to carry the day's thought?
Did you resist it?
Did it make you feel uneasy?
Did it bring you comfort?
Here are Jesus' own words: "Unless you become
as a little child you can not enter the kingdom of God."
Was there a time today when you ran to God/Mother?
Was there a time when you might have?
Look back over your life.
Was there a time
when you did not feel immediately consoled,
but now can see
that this provided an opportunity for growth?

Night Prayer

Mother Jesus,
you will never allow us, your children, to perish.
Let me sense your constant presence and care.
Help me to trust
that I have your mercy and compassion
and that all that happens
transpires for my own good.

DAY TWENTY-TWO

MY DAY BEGINS

In our true Mother, Jesus,
our life is grounded in uncreated wisdom
that foresees all,
along with the Father's almighty power
and the Holy Spirit's sovereign goodness.
By taking upon himself our nature,
he restored us to life.
By dying upon the cross,
he carried us to eternal life.
From that moment until the end of time,
he nurtures and helps us on,
just as the great loving concern of motherhood wishes
and the natural need of the child desires.
Beautiful and sweet
is our heavenly mother in the sight of our spirits,
and in the sight of our heavenly mother.
Dear and beautiful are her gracious children,
gentle and humble as children innately are.
For by nature,
the child does not despair of the mother's love.

Nor by nature does a child try to be self-reliant.
A mother instinctively loves the child
and this child, in turn, loves her.
These beautiful qualities and many others
please and serve our heavenly Mother.
There is, in this life,
no higher state than childhood,
with its weakness and helplessness and ignorance,
until our gracious Mother
brings us up into our Father's joy.
In that joy,
we will truly be shown what he means
by the sweet words:
"All will be well,
and you yourself shall see
that every manner of thing
will be well."

ALL THROUGH THE DAY

There is, in this life, no higher state than childhood.

MY DAY IS ENDING

How has Mother God fed and fostered you today?
What is it like to try to live as a child of God?
How is it easy?
Difficult?
Satisfying?
Humbling?
How have you been able to rely upon Mother today?
How might you have relied more upon her?

NIGHT PRAYER

Lovely Mother,
help me to relax into the state of being a child.
Let me rely upon you for my well-being,
and make me run to you for comfort.
May I feel my helplessness
and rejoice in your presence,
knowing that you will lift me up
into our Father's bliss.

DAY TWENTY-THREE

My Day Begins

And then our good Lord opened my spiritual eye,
and showed me my spirit
in the middle of my heart.
I saw the soul as wide
as if it were an unlimited realm.
It also resembled a blessed kingdom.
Indeed it was a wondrous city
in whose center sits our Lord, Jesus,
handsome and tall.
And he is magnificently clothed in glory.
In rightful peace and rest,
he assumes his seat in our spirits.
And from this seat,
he has dominion over everything in creation.
Never will he abandon this seat
that he has taken in our spirits,
for he has made his home and
eternal dwelling within us.
That he has done this shows the joy God has
in the creation of our spirits.

For as wonderfully as any creature could be formed
does the Father as well as the Son and the Holy Spirit
wish our spirit to be fashioned.
And so we are made.
From this I came to see
that the spirit can never rest
in anything lower than itself.
And when it rises above all creation into itself,
it still finds no satisfaction remaining so,
for its sight is wondrously set upon God.
God is the Creator dwelling within us, and
within the human soul is God's true abode.
And when our soul realizes this,
it becomes like the one it beholds
and grace quietly unites it to God in peace.

ALL THROUGH THE DAY

He has made his home and eternal dwelling within us.

MY DAY IS ENDING

What lifted your soul up to God today?
Have there been times today
when you felt the presence of Jesus within you?

Were there times
when you did not sense his presence?
How have you experienced God's delight in you today?

NIGHT PRAYER

Lord Jesus,
I am honored
to have you make my spirit your dwelling place.
Help me to appreciate your delight in me.
May my actions toward my neighbors
always mirror your love.

MY DAY BEGINS

God opened my spiritual sight
and showed me my spirit in my heart.
The spirit is as large as an eternal world
and a blessed realm as well.
And the greatest light
and the brightest shining in the city of spirit
is God's glorious love.
What can allow us to take more delight in God
than to see that he takes delight in us,
the greatest of all his creatures?
In this same vision I saw
that if the blessed Trinity could have made our spirit
any better, more beautiful, or more noble,
God would not have been pleased and satisfied
with our creation.
But because God has made us
so beautiful, so good, and so precious,
God is infinitely delighted in the creation of our spirit.
And the Trinity wishes us
to be transported up above this world

and all its empty suffering,
to delight in God.
This delicious revelation is without end.
And God would like us to rest in it
while we are still on earth.
For when we contemplate God
we are made like unto God.
And through grace we are united in his peace.
That I saw God sitting gave me special delight,
for sitting implies sure confidence
and an eternal dwelling of rest.
God assured me that it was indeed he
who had shown me all of this.

ALL THROUGH THE DAY

When we contemplate God we are made like unto God.

MY DAY IS ENDING

Spend some time now simply resting in the Lord.
Imagine Jesus seated in your heart,
and simply be aware
of any feelings or sensations that arise.

NIGHT PRAYER

Gracious Lord,
thank you for showing me
the delight you take in me.
You give me great joy in turn
because you choose to make of me your home.
May my contemplation of you
make me more like you
and increase my own joy
in your glorious creation.

MY DAY BEGINS

God showed me two kinds of spiritual sickness.
They are spiritual blindness and physical sloth.
To help us with this, Our Lord showed
how patiently he endured his suffering
and how he took joy and delight in that passion
because he loved us.
He offered this as an example
so that we might endure our pains
with joy and wisdom.
Our pains currently oppress us
because we are ignorant of love.
We worry about our past
and are consumed with guilt for what we have done.
But God wants us
to see and delight in everything through love.
Some people believe God is omnipotent
and may do everything.
Others think that he is all-wise and can do everything,
but we fail to believe
that he is all-wise and will do everything.

Our ignorance of this
is the greatest obstacle for God's lovers.
For even when we begin to hate sin,
we still bear a fear which works against us.
We become so dejected and depressed
that we are beyond comfort.
We mistake this dread for humility,
but this is horribly blind and weak.
God wills that, of all the qualities of the blessed Trinity,
we should be most certain of
and take most delight in his love.
Love brings power and wisdom down to our level.
When we repent,
God forgets our sins through his courtesy.
So too, he wants us also to forget our sins
and leave behind
both depression and anxiety.

ALL THROUGH THE DAY

God wants us to forget our sin.

MY DAY IS ENDING

How have you found delight in love today?
How did you experience God's love for you today?

Spend a few moments imagining your imperfections,
failures, and sins that have been forgotten
in God's love.

NIGHT PRAYER

Jesus Lord,
I take delight in your love.
Increase my faith in that love
so that I may let go of all fear and depression.
With your love assured,
nothing is strong enough
to come between us.

MY DAY BEGINS

I saw that God can take care of us completely.
And there are three things that we truly need,
and these three things bring us to languish in love.
The first is love.
The others are the languishing of love
and the compassion of love.
Love's compassion protects us during our time of need,
and love's languish draws us up to heaven.
God is thirsty and wants
everyone to be drawn up to him.
That thirst has drawn his holy ones into bliss.
He always draws and drinks,
attracting his beloved,
and still he thirsts and languishes.
I see three ways that God languishes,
but all of these modes have the same purpose.
First he desires to teach us
to know and love him more and more.
That suits us and is to our gain.

Second, he desires us to share in his bliss
as happens with those
taken out of affliction and into heaven.
Third, he desires to fill us with his bliss
as will happen on the last day
when we will be filled with everlasting happiness.
I saw as I knew from faith
that pain and suffering will end
for those who are saved.
And not only shall we receive that same happiness
which those in heaven already have,
but a new one as well.
This happiness will flow from God abundantly
and fill us to the brim.

All Through the Day

God is thirsty and wants everyone to be drawn
up to him.

My Day Is Ending

Spend some time imagining God's longing for you.
Can you sense the urgency, the yearning
of God's love?

When have you felt a longing for God today?
How has the thought of God's love for you
helped you through hard times today?

NIGHT PRAYER

Courteous Lord,
teach me the extent of your delight in me.
Make me feel your love constantly.
Lift me out of my sorrow
and into the bliss of knowing
how much you care for me.
And help me to share your love
with everyone I meet.

DAY TWENTY-SEVEN

My Day Begins

For God says:
"Do not accuse yourself too much
or think that your distress and woe is due to
your fault."
Whatever you do, suffering will be your lot.
This place is a prison, and life a penance.
But that penance need not be in vain,
and we rejoice already in the cure.
And the cure is that God is with us
Guarding us and guiding us into the fullness of joy.
There is unending joy knowing that God,
our protector here,
will be our bliss hereafter.
God is our way, our destination in true love,
and our sure trust.
So let us fly to the Lord,
so that we may be comforted.
Let us touch him so that we might be cleansed;
let us cling to him, so that we may be safe from
every danger.

Our courteous Lord wishes us
to be as at ease with him
as heart may think or soul desire;
But let us not ease into this familiarity so casually
that we forget our own courtesy.
For God himself is supremely friendly
and as courteous as he is friendly;
indeed he is courtesy itself.
And he wants his loved ones
to be like himself in every way,
and to be perfectly like our Lord
is true salvation
and supreme joy.

ALL THROUGH THE DAY

The cure is that God is with us.

MY DAY IS ENDING

How has the knowledge that God is with you
helped you through this day?
Are there times when you have forgotten
the thought for the day?

If so, remember those times now
and bring the thought that God is with you
into the situation.
How does it change things?
What happened to you
today that you might call profitable penance?
Does it help you to think in this way?

NIGHT PRAYER

Courteous Lover,
thank you for your presence throughout the day.
Help me to see that everything leads to you
and that you lead me toward the bliss
you wish me to enjoy.
Let me to share your love with my neighbors.
May they see how your courtesy lifts me up,
and may they sense in me
your love for all creatures.

My Day Begins

God wants us to know four things:
First, he is the ground from whom
we derive our life and our very existence.
Second, he protects us with strength and mercy
while we are in sin,
in the midst of our savage foes.
We jeopardize ourselves
because we give them the opportunity to attack us,
and we are unaware of our need.
Third, he courteously safeguards us
and alerts us when we go awry.
Fourth, with forbearance, God waits for us
and does not grow angry or sullen,
because above all God wants us to turn to him
and become united to him through love,
as he already is linked to us.
Through insight and grace
we become aware of our sin,
but such awareness does not harm us
or make us abandon hope.

For through this lowly knowledge
we will be sifted out from whatever is not of God
through remorse and grace.
In the end, Jesus will heal us totally
and join us to him.
He has had the foresight
to provide this breaking and healing for everyone,
so that the greatest of saints
may see their sinfulness and need along with me.
And I, the least of God's people,
find comfort along with the greatest.
So God joins us in charity.

All Through the Day

We are unaware of our need.

My Day Is Ending

How have you experienced God's presence
with you today?
Have you felt God's protection?
God's mercy?
God's cure?
God's courtesy?

Have you come to knowledge today of your frailty
and sinfulness?
Have you experienced your need?
If so, take it to God in prayer.

NIGHT PRAYER

Dear Lord,
be with me
as my foundation and hope.
Protect me when I err and stray.
Lift me when I fall down.
Help me to know my need
and teach me to turn only to you
for solace.

MY DAY BEGINS

We are guided in this transitory life
by God our Father
who is endless day.
In this light, Christ our Mother and the Holy Spirit
conduct us.
God shines forth this light with providence,
making it available to us
in the nighttime of our need.
The light makes possible our life.
Our pain and sorrow derive from the night.
But God is with us even in dejection,
for we believe in the light
thanks to his mercy and grace,
and we walk in it
with wisdom and strength.
At sorrow's end
our eyes will be opened;
we shall see clearly
that the light shines with fullness;

for this light is our God
shining through Jesus our Savior.
This light is charity,
and God's wisdom measures it out
for our well being.
It is not yet bright enough
for us to see the day of our happiness,
nor is it completely hidden from us.
But it is a light
in which we can profitably live
and strive to receive the everlasting glory of God
So faith and hope
lead us to love
and in the end,
all will be love.

ALL THROUGH THE DAY

In the end everything will be love.

MY DAY IS ENDING

When has the light of faith appeared in your life today?
Did you recognize it as such at the time?
Looking back now:
are there times during which it shined unrecognized?

Where has charity been manifested today?
How have you experienced charity from God?
How have you shown God's charity to others?

Night Prayer

Courteous Lord,
this day closes,
and night draws on.
Help me to find your light in the darkness.
Keep me aware of your loving presence.
Lead me with gentleness to faith,
and from faith to hope,
and help me see that all leads
only to charity and love.

DAY THIRTY

My Day Begins

I beheld and understood
that faith is our light in the darkness,
which light is God, our eternal day.
This light is charity,
and God's wisdom measures it out to us for our good.
It is not so dazzling
that we can at present behold our day of happiness,
nor is it hidden from us.
Rather it is a light in which we can live profitably,
meriting God's gratitude for our work.
I came to see this when he said to me,
"Thank you for your service and your labor."
At this sight I was filled with wonder.
For in spite of our folly and blindness in this life,
our courteous Lord has concern for us,
and rejoices in his labors in our spirits.
And we can please him
by believing him in wisdom and truth,
and rejoicing with him and in him.
For as we shall blissfully join God

for all eternity in praise and thanks,
so indeed we have been known and loved
in his intention from before the creation.
In this ceaseless love, he first made us;
in this same love, he guards us
and saves us from any hurt
which might forfeit our happiness.
So when we are finally brought face to face with God,
we shall behold in God with clarity, and
the mysteries presently concealed
from us will be uncovered.
And no one will want to say then,
"Lord, if only things were different,
it would have been well."
Rather shall we shout with one accord,
"Lord, blessed be your name!
For whatever is, is good.
And now we see indeed
that everything has happened as planned by you
before anything was made."

All Through the Day

Everything has happened as planned by you
before anything was made.

MY DAY IS ENDING

Recollect the presence of faith in your life today.
What is it like?
How does it affect the way you live?
How might its increase
change the way you experience life?
How have you experienced God's concern for your
well-being today?
Looking back, can you discern moments when you
were unaware of it, or even despaired of it?
Spend a few minutes with the last few lines of today's
reading. Sit with them before you.
If a phrase or a word strikes you, linger over it.
Simply remain in relaxation and joy as these
last words from Julian give you hope.

NIGHT PRAYER

Lord, increase my faith and trust
in your good intentions for us.
Help me to go about my life confident
that whatever happens to me
will ultimately work out for the best,
and help me to praise your goodness
in all times and places.

ONE FINAL WORD

This book was created to be nothing more than a gateway—a gateway to the spiritual wisdom of a specific teacher, and a gateway opening on your own spiritual path.

You may decide that Julian of Norwich is someone whose experience of God is one that you wish to follow more closely and deeply. In that case, you should get a copy of the entire text of *Showings* and pray it as you have prayed this gateway retreat.

You may decide that Julian's experience has not helped you. There are many other teachers. Somewhere, there is the right teacher for your own, very special, absolutely unique journey of the spirit. You will find your teacher; you will discover your path. We would not be searching, as St. Augustine reminds us, if we had not already been found.